REBELLION AND UNION IN THE CANADAS

Douglas Baldwin

Weigl

CALGARY
www.weigl.com

We acknowledge the financial support of the Government of Canada through the Book Publishing Industry Development Program (BPIDP) for our publishing activities.

Published by Weigl Educational Publishers Limited
6325 – 10 Street SE
Calgary, Alberta, Canada
T2H 2Z9

Web site: www.weigl.com

National Library of Canada Cataloguing-in-Publication Data

Baldwin, Douglas, 1944-
   Rebellion and union in the Canadas / Douglas Baldwin.

(Canadian history)
Includes bibliographical references and index.
Interest grade level: For use in grades 6-8.
ISBN 1-55388-013-7 (hardcover) ISBN 1-55388-086-2 (softcover)

   1. Canada--History--Rebellion, 1837-1838--Juvenile literature.
2. Canada--History--1841-1867--Juvenile literature. I. Title. II. Series: Canadian history (Calgary, Alta.)

FC450.B34 2002   971.03'8   C2002-901450-6   F1032.B34 2002

Printed in the United States of America
2 3 4 5 6 7 8 9 0   06 05

Project Coordinator
Michael Lowry
Editor
Lynn Hamilton
Copy Editor
Diana Marshall
Photo Researcher
Gayle Murdoff
Designer
Warren Clark
Layout
Terry Paulhus

CONTENTS

Setting the Stage for REBELLION

By the 1830s, people in both Canadas had become increasingly discontented.

The Constitutional Act of 1791 introduced representative government and distinct French and British societies in the Canadas. After the American Revolution, many Loyalists immigrated to the colony of Québec. They were undeniably loyal to Britain, having proven their support by sacrificing their homes and families in the revolution. Despite the immigration of the Loyalists, the majority of the colony's population was still French Canadian. If Britain granted representative government, the French would be unable to vote. They were Roman Catholic, so could not swear loyalty to the king, who was head of the **Anglican Church**.

The Constitutional Act divided the colony of Québec into two provinces—Upper Canada and Lower Canada. This division separated the French Canadians, who lived mainly in Lower Canada, from most of the British, who lived mainly in

FURTHER UNDERSTANDING

American Revolution Also known as the American War of Independence (1775–1783), the American Revolution was the struggle through which the **Thirteen Colonies** won independence from Britain. Discontent had been increasing for years in the American colonies as they chafed under British control of their economy and administration. In 1775, resentment finally erupted into war. The Thirteen Colonies officially declared their independence in 1776 with the Declaration of Independence.

Constitutional Act The Constitutional Act of 1791 replaced the Québec Act of 1774. The Québec Act acknowledged that the majority of Québec's population was French by officially allowing the French Canadians to maintain many aspects of their lifestyle. The Constitutional Act was Britain's response to the immigration of the Loyalists, which made it impossible for them not to grant representative government.

Loyalists The Loyalists were American colonists who supported Britain during the American Revolution. They did not want independence, wishing instead, to remain tied to the British Empire. Most Loyalists were farmers. They came from a variety of ethnic backgrounds, including recent European immigrants, free African Americans, escaped slaves, and Aboriginal peoples. After Britain's defeat, the Loyalists found life in the United States intolerable. Many were placed in prison, denied civil rights, and had their property confiscated. About 40,000 to 50,000 Loyalists fled to Canada after the revolution. Britain did its best to recognize their loyalty. Free land was their main reward. Their **conservative** political views were very influential in Canada's political development, mainly in their rejection of revolution as a means of settling conflict.

Representative government In a representative government, the population elects individuals to make laws on their behalf. The elected individuals represent the interests of the people who elected them. For a large population, this system is more efficient than **direct democracy**.

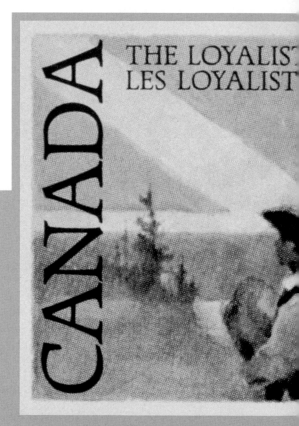

■ On July 3, 1984, Canada Post issued a stamp commemorating the people who remained loyal to Great Britain during the American Revolution.

Upper Canada. Each province had its own representative assembly. The act also gave Roman Catholics the right to vote and to hold office. Upper Canada maintained British laws, including existing property laws. Lower Canada combined French land and civil laws with British criminal laws. The arrival of the Loyalists guaranteed that Canada would have a strong British population. The act satisfied the demands of both the French and the British.

While the Constitutional Act granted the colonies representative government, the powers of the Assemblies were intentionally limited. Britain feared that, with greater powers, the colonies might seek independence as had the American colonies. Upper Canadians were satisfied with the changes, and Lower Canadians quickly adapted to the representational assembly, which for them was a new institution. The laws set by the Constitutional Act governed the colonies for many years. By the 1830s, people in both Canadas had become increasingly discontented. The Canadas were poised for rebellion.

■■ Upper Canada's first legislature met in 1782.

CANADA INVADED!
The War of 1812

Sir Isaac Brock had reason to worry—he had only 1,500 regular soldiers.

On June 18, 1812, American president James Madison declared war on Britain, thus beginning the War of 1812. The Americans were angered by the British navy's searches of American ships for British deserters. At one point, the British mistakenly seized American sailors. This action interfered with American trade with France, which was then at war with Britain. Americans were also eager to obtain the land reserved by Britain for its Aboriginal allies.

Since Britain's navy was considered unbeatable, the Americans began the war by attacking Upper Canada. One American politician declared, "We have the Canadas as much under our command as Great Britain has the ocean … I would take the whole continent from her and ask no favours. I wish never to see peace till we do."

The Americans were confident they would succeed. The citizens of the United States outnumbered the residents of **British North America** by 8 million to 500,000. In addition, many settlers had recently moved to Canada from the United States and might welcome the invaders.

In Upper Canada, Sir Isaac Brock had reason to worry. He had only 1,500 regular soldiers, although he also had Aboriginal

FURTHER UNDERSTANDING

Sir Isaac Brock Born in 1769, Sir Isaac Brock is considered a hero and saviour of Upper Canada. His strategies during the war were bold, courageous, and inspirational. Brock needed a victory to give the people hope. The British captures of Fort Michilimackinac and Detroit early in the war encouraged Canadian settlers to join the militia.

In October 1812, Brock rushed his troops to the Niagara River, successfully repelling the American invasion at Queenston Heights. In his officer's hat, red coat, and white trousers, Brock was an easy target. He was shot and killed as he led a charge of soldiers up the hill.

Queenston Heights On October 13, 1812, New York's state militia launched an attack before dawn and seized control of a strategic spot at Queenston Heights. As the British fought to regain their position, Sir Isaac Brock and his **aide-de-camp**, Lieutenant-Colonel John Macdonnell, were killed. Eventually Major-General Roger Hale Sheaffe attacked from behind and took almost 1,000

American militiamen prisoner. During the battle, the vastly outnumbered British forces lost 28 soldiers, with 77 injured.

Tecumseh Tecumseh was a Shawnee nation chief who tried to form an alliance of Aboriginal groups to halt American territorial expansion. His participation in the War of 1812 helped Brock win the victory at Detroit and several later victories against the Americans. During the battle of Moraviantown on October 5, 1813, Tecumseh was killed after the British forces fled. His death ended the co-ordinated Aboriginal resistance to the Americans south of the Great Lakes.

War of 1812 The Americans were confident when entering the war. Britain was busy fighting France. It seemed that without strong British support, the Canadian colonies would quickly succumb to American forces. Thomas Jefferson remarked that the capture of Canada was "a mere matter of marching." He was proven wrong by the events of the three-year-long battle.

■ In 1824, Brock's body was moved to the summit of Queenston Heights and buried under a monument created in his honour. It was destroyed in 1840, but was replaced in 1853 by another monument that can still be seen today.

allies, such as Tecumseh of the Shawnee nation. Many settlers believed Canada would be defeated quickly and refused to volunteer to fight. "Most people have lost all confidence," Brock wrote. "I, however, speak loudly and look big."

A Slow, Bloody Victory

The war was brutal. After the Americans captured and destroyed York—present-day Toronto—in 1813, an American doctor recorded the battle's aftermath:

Nothing but the groans of the wounded and agonies of the dying are to be heard. The surgeon wading in blood, cutting off arms, legs … to hear the poor creatures crying "Oh, my God, my God! Doctor! Doctor! Cut off my leg relieve me from misery! I can't live, I can't live" would have rent a heart of steel … I cut and slashed for forty-eight hours without food or sleep.

The war lasted almost three years. Canadian and British soldiers more than held their own. In general, the war was a long series of blunders and poor strategies. The indecisive struggle ended with the Treaty of Ghent in 1814.

The primary impact of the war on British North America was the increase in provincial pride. Canadians had fought together against a common enemy. Those who remained in Canada did so because they wished to keep ties with Britain.

LAURA SECORD

Laura Secord was born in Massachusetts in 1775. She moved to Canada when she was 20 years old. During the War of 1812, she overheard American officers discussing their plan to attack a British post at Beaver Dam. She snuck away from her home in Queenston, on the Niagara River. She trekked 32 kilometres, detouring through forests and trees to avoid American lines. She informed British Lieutenant James FitzGibbon of the upcoming attack.

The Americans were taken by surprise two days later, when an Aboriginal and British force ambushed them. The Americans surrendered.

When her story was heard and verified by FitzGibbon, Secord became a Canadian heroine. Almost fifty years after her dangerous trek, she received a monetary award from the Prince of Wales. Today, Secord is remembered by monuments at Queenston Heights and Niagara Falls.

■ The British, Aboriginal, and Canadian forces won the battle at Queenston Heights. The victory gave the Canadians confidence that they could resist the larger American army.

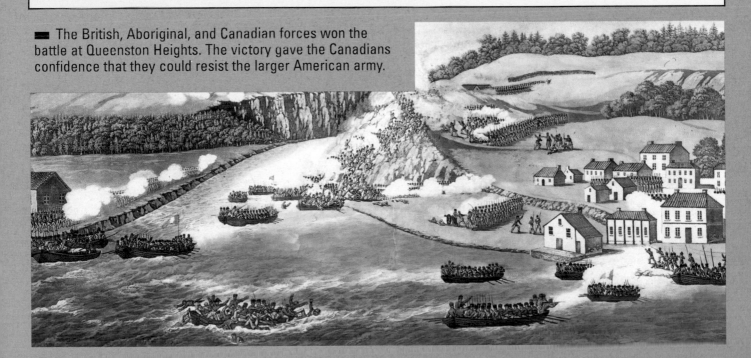

GOVERNMENT
in British North America

The Constitutional Act of 1791 brought representative government to the Canadas, but not responsible government. The governments of the Canadas still reflected the interests of Britain more often than the interests of the inhabitants of the colonies.

Each colony in British North America had a similar form of government. At the head of Lower Canada was a governor, while Upper Canada was led by a lieutenant-governor. These positions were appointed and could be removed only by the British government. These officials had more power in the colony than the monarch had in Britain. Bills could not become laws until they signed them. They also decided when elections would be held. Britain could veto or reject any law passed by the colony within two years.

The Executive and Legislative Councils were the most important political bodies in British North America. The Legislative Council drew up laws that the lieutenant-governor would pass. The Executive Council advised the lieutenant-governor and carried out the laws. The governor appointed the members of the Legislative and Executive Councils. The legislative councillors kept their positions for life. The executive councillors kept their positions as long as the lieutenant-governor was pleased with their work. The two councils worked closely together, and some people sat on both councils. Most councillors were chosen from among the wealthy, well-educated citizens of the colony.

The Assembly was the least important political body in the colonies. Each colony was divided into voting districts that elected representatives to its Assembly. The Assembly raised money through taxes and drew up bills for the colony. These bills did not become laws until they were approved by the Legislative Council and signed by the lieutenant-governor. Once approved and signed, the bill became an Act.

■ Most of the Loyalist women who came to the Canadas could spin, and some could weave. Flax was grown to provide fibre for linen, and sheep were raised for wool.

FURTHER UNDERSTANDING

Responsible government

Responsible government generally means that the government is responsible to the people. However, as it developed in Canada, responsible government came to mean that the government—the Executive Council—is responsible to the representatives of the people. These representatives are elected by the people to form the Assembly. Under responsible government, if the majority of the representatives in the Assembly do not approve of the actions of the Executive Council, it could force the council members to resign. Then, either a new Executive Council would be appointed by the Assembly, or there would be an election. The elected representatives were to be responsible to the voters, while the Executive Council would be responsible to the elected politicians. Today, the cabinet and the prime minister are responsible to the House of Commons.

THE RIGHT TO VOTE

During the nineteenth century, citizens of British North America viewed the **franchise** differently than most Canadians would today. At the time, Canada was not a democratic nation in the way that democracy is understood today. The men who governed the country did not believe in universal **suffrage**. The only people allowed to elect representatives to government were men, 21 years of age or older, who owned a certain amount of land. Thus only wealthy males could be elected to Parliament. Women, children, criminals, the poor, and Aboriginal peoples were all denied the franchise.

George Brown was a landowner and publisher of the *Toronto Globe* newspaper. He believed that only the wealthy, educated men of the country were capable of understanding the problems of government. If the "ignorant, unreasoning masses" were allowed to vote, he argued, then the politicians would be forced to do what the "ignorant" people wanted in order to be elected. If this happened he cautioned, the wealthy would soon "sink to the level of the masses."

Brown believed that people who owned property were superior because they owned a part of the country. He believed they should have a voice in government decisions. The interests of those who did not own property would be looked after by people who were intelligent enough to know exactly what would be best for all.

GOVERNMENT IN BRITISH NORTH AMERICA, 1791–1848

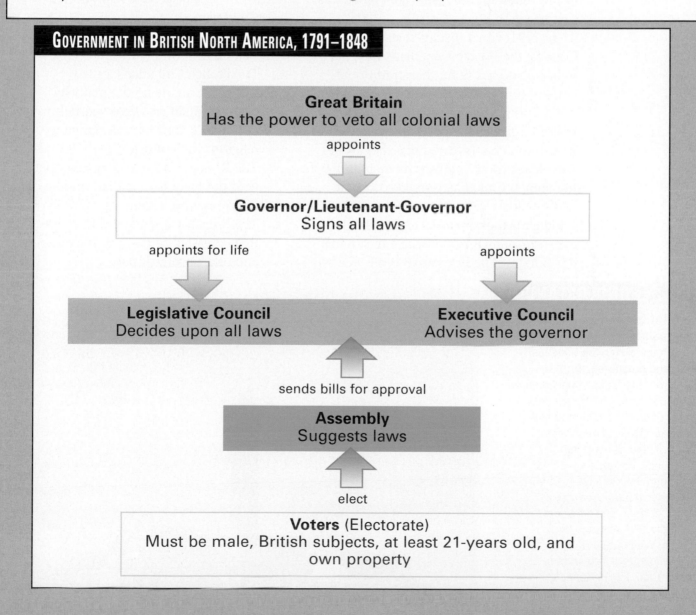

Great Britain
Has the power to veto all colonial laws

appoints

Governor/Lieutenant-Governor
Signs all laws

appoints for life   appoints

Legislative Council
Decides upon all laws

Executive Council
Advises the governor

sends bills for approval

Assembly
Suggests laws

elect

Voters (Electorate)
Must be male, British subjects, at least 21-years old, and own property

Rumbles of **DISCONTENT**

In the first decades of the 1800s, people began to feel that their representative system was unjust. Often, the governor and his councillors did not approve the bills recommended by the Assembly. Faced with one of the Assembly's bills, they often tossed it out or rewrote it to suit their own needs. Hostility toward the government system began to grow in both colonies. Groups promoting reform became more radical and active as the 1830s approached. Open rebellions first began in Lower Canada.

In 1791, when Britain created Lower Canada, the French Canadians were happy to be able to maintain their traditional landholding system and French civil law. In addition, Roman Catholics were able to hold office in the government and vote. British merchants feared that they would soon lose power in government, and that the French Canadians would control it.

Only forty years later, the French Canadians took up arms against 1791's constitution, while the British merchants defended it. The Legislative and Executive Councils were typically composed of British citizens and supporters of Britain. The Assembly consisted mostly of French-Canadian members. As a result, the councils and the Assembly had different priorities. Since the councils could block the initiatives of the Assembly, the Assembly lacked the power needed to make changes.

Lower Canadian society could be divided into four major groups. Each one of these four groups had different goals and values.

1. The British settlers and merchants wanted to promote business.
2. The French Canadians, called habitants, made up the majority of the population. They wanted to preserve their lifestyle, language, religion, and culture.
3. The Roman Catholic clergy competed with the French-Canadian middle class to represent the habitants.
4. The French-Canadian middle class, that consisted of doctors, lawyers, and other professionals.

FURTHER UNDERSTANDING

Population During the forty years following the Constitutional Act, the Canadas grew and prospered. Both colonies experienced population increases. Immigrants came to Upper Canada from Europe and America. While Upper Canada was still mainly a farming community, its settlers wanted to expand their economy. Lower Canada had flourished into a centre of trade and commerce along the St. Lawrence River system. While Upper Canada's population grew mainly from immigration, Lower Canada's population increase was due to its high birth rate.

■ When Montréal was declared a city in 1831, it had surpassed Québec as the largest city in Canada. It was the capital of Canada from 1844 to 1849.

The British MERCHANTS

British merchants made up an influential segment of society in Lower Canada. The typical merchant was an English-speaking Protestant living in Montréal or Québec City. Merchants were generally prosperous and made their money importing manufactured goods and exporting timber, wheat, and flour. To move these goods to the markets, merchants wanted the colony to improve transportation along the St. Lawrence River by building canals. They believed that these public works should be paid for by taxing farmland.

The British merchants felt that the habitants were not growing as much wheat as they should. Some British merchants bought their own **seigneuries**, and the governor gave them additional land. The merchants encouraged British immigrants to settle in Lower Canada to support their economic plans and help produce more wheat. Some British citizens wanted to assimilate all French Canadians into British culture.

In 1791, British merchants dominated the Assembly and were able to do as they wished. One decade later, after French Canadians were given the right to vote and hold office, they took control of the Assembly.

The French Canadians did not support the British merchants' business plans. As a result, the merchants turned to the governor for support. The governor appointed many British merchants to the Legislative Council. He also gave their children high-paying and influential civil service jobs. This enabled the merchants to control important decisions.

> In 1791, British merchants dominated the Assembly.

■ The St. Lawrence River canal was the first lock canal in North America. It was designed and built by Captain William Twiss in Coteau-du-Lac, Québec. Construction took place between 1770 and 1780.

The HABITANTS

Good farmland was becoming scarce and many habitants worried that their sons would not be able to have their own land.

Nine out of every ten French Canadians were farmers, or habitants. They were mainly Roman Catholics, and few spoke any English. Their high birth rate caused the French-Canadian population to increase from 161,000 in 1790 to 650,000 in 1837. As a result, good quality farmland was becoming scarce, and many habitants worried that their sons would not be able to have their own land. Their worry increased when the governor granted some of the best farmland to British merchants, army officers, and council members.

Times were not good for the habitant. The timber trade began to decline in the 1830s. In addition, the habitants' ancestors had tilled the soil for generations, exhausting the land. Diseases, such as **wheat rust**, spread rapidly and ruined crops. There were crop failures in Lower Canada in 1826, 1827, 1832, and 1833. The small amount of wheat harvested was sold at low prices. Many farmers barely grew enough to feed their families. Eventually, wheat, along with other foods, had to be purchased from farmers in Upper Canada.

To make matters worse, emigrants from Britain flooded into Lower Canada after the War of 1812. Between 1832 and 1834, some of these new arrivals brought cholera. There was no known cure for this disease and it caused a painful death. In 1832, about 7,000 French Canadians died from cholera. The public was dissatisfied with the way the government handled the cholera epidemic. By the end of the 1830s, the habitants were anxious for change.

■ Wealthy habitants dressed in elegant clothing similar to that worn in France. However, by the time the clothes arrived in Canada, they were already out of style in France, since ships sailed from Europe only once each year.

FURTHER UNDERSTANDING

Cholera An intestinal disorder, cholera is associated with unsanitary living conditions. It results when human waste contaminates food and water supplies. If treated, cholera will last a few days, but when left untreated, it can lead to death.

Before cholera was fully understood, it was widely feared. At the time, no cure existed, and no one knew how it was transmitted. When an epidemic struck, a town would impose a **quarantine** to help prevent the spread of the disease. At the time, most people believed that foul air caused diseases. During the cholera epidemic of 1832, some cities burned barrels of tar in the streets in the belief that it would cleanse the atmosphere.

The Roman Catholic CLERGY

The clergy was caught between the needs of the habitants and the demands of the British rulers. As most priests came from farming families, they understood the habitants' problems. They promoted farming and believed French Canadians should leave business to the British merchants. At the same time, the clergy had connections with the governor and the Executive and Legislative Councils. The Roman Catholic church was against violence, and did not approve of democracy.

The Roman Catholic church was important to life in Lower Canada. It cared for the poor, orphaned, or old of the colony. The church operated the hospitals and ran the schools. The clergy used its position of influence to convince people to retain their French language, religion, and lifestyle. The English language was rarely taught.

The Roman Catholic church did not have as much power as it wanted. The average priest was overworked and had little time to influence politics. In 1760, there was one priest for every 350 people. By 1830, only one priest served every 1,800 French Canadians.

> The clergy used its position of influence to convince people to retain their French language, religion, and lifestyle.

■ Notre Dame des Victoires, a small church in Québec City, was built in 1690. The church was given its name after the French defended Québec against the English a few years later.

French-Canadian Middle CLASS

The French-Canadian educational system trained so many lawyers and doctors that they had trouble making a living.

The French-Canadian middle class consisted of lawyers, doctors, and journalists. They were well-educated and many spoke English. Although they were Roman Catholics, the middle class competed with the clergy for the support of French Canadians.

The French-Canadian educational system trained so many lawyers and doctors that they had trouble making a living. Part of the problem was that the habitants were too poor to pay for their services. To gain respect and prestige in the community, some French-Canadian professionals ran for election in the Assembly.

Soon, the French-Canadian middle class dominated the Assembly. Led by Louis-Joseph Papineau, they formed a political party called the Parti Patriote. The Patriotes wanted to preserve French-Canadian ways, including the seigneurial system, Roman Catholicism, French civil laws, and the French language. To achieve these goals, the Patriotes wanted the Assembly to have control over the Executive and Legislative Councils. They wanted the Assembly to have the power to make the laws for the colony, so they demanded responsible government.

FURTHER UNDERSTANDING

Parti Patriote Called the *Parti Canadien* until 1826, the Parti Patriote first became popular with the habitants because it supported opening new seigneuries. Its main supporters were French Canadians who distrusted British rule. The Parti Patriote also earned the support of educated French professionals and the elite, who opposed the appointed councils. When the Parti Patriote finally dominated the Assembly, it was repeatedly blocked by the Executive and Legislative Councils. Despite this, the Assembly did manage to reduce some of the power of the councils by voting against changes promoted by the British merchants, such as the building of canals.

Petition A group can make a formal request to a person or group in authority—such as the ruling government—in the form of a petition. Often in writing, it requests a change or form of action. People are sometimes asked to sign their names to show their support for the request.

Seigneurial system The French landholding system, called the seigneurial system, granted land to important people, who were then responsible for parcelling out long narrow strips of land along rivers to settlers. They also collected rents and taxes. It was different from the British freehold system in which a person had the legal right, or deed, to a piece of land for the duration of their lifetime. A British landholder could sell the land or pass it on to their heirs. Women rarely held property deeds. Even if a woman did hold land, she often did not vote. Voting was considered a male privilege.

■ Seigneuries were usually divided into river lots. This system allowed multiple access to the river. Although the Parti Patriote fought to maintain the seigneurial system of land distribution, it was abolished in 1854.

LOUIS-JOSEPH PAPINEAU

Louis-Joseph Papineau led the movement for reform in Lower Canada. Born in Montréal in 1786, Papineau trained to be a lawyer. He did not enjoy law and only practised it occasionally. In 1809, he was elected to the Assembly in Lower Canada. Papineau was an eloquent speaker, which led to his being named speaker of the Assembly in 1815. That same year, he became the leader of the Parti Patriote.

Papineau began his political career as an admirer of Britain. He supported the British army against the American invaders in 1812. At first, he sought reform through peaceful, democratic means. He wrote letters and organized petitions to the British government.

When his efforts failed, Papineau became anti-British and turned to American ideas for inspiration. His actions became more radical during the 1820s and 1830s. He encouraged his supporters to stop paying taxes and avoid projects that would benefit the British minority. He started a campaign to discourage people from buying British goods.

Papineau was a seigneur and a strong supporter of the old social order in French Canada. He wanted to make Lower Canada into a French-speaking, American-style democracy. He idealized a separate, independent French-Canadian country, in which the majority of the citizens would be moral, hard-working farmers.

At home on his seigneury, Papineau avoided interaction with people. When invited to balls, he often retired to a back room and played chess. He disliked politics, yet felt it was his duty to help his people. At the same time, he was ambitious and vain. Although he could be difficult to deal with, Papineau had a charismatic personality and a great deal of charm. Some habitants talked about making him king, while others considered him the one who would free French Canadians from British rule.

■ Louis-Joseph Papineau was an aristocrat who fought for both radical reforms and to preserve traditional French-Canadian values.

REBELLION in Lower Canada

The Patriotes began printing their own money and wrote a declaration of independence.

By 1830, the battle lines had been drawn. On one side was the Patriote-led Assembly, which represented the majority of the population in Lower Canada. This side was angry that the councils held much of the political power of the colony. The Patriotes received support from Irish farmers, who disliked British rule, and from British settlers with democratic ideals.

The Assembly stood in opposition to the elite group called the Château Clique, whose members sat in the two councils. Many members of the Château Clique were merchants who governed for their own self-interests. Between 1822 and 1836, the Legislative Council rejected 234 bills proposed by the Assembly.

When Papineau recruited 88,000 people to sign a petition demanding changes, Governor Lord Aylmer mocked the petition. Since 77,000 of these signatures were made with a cross, he called the petitioners the "knights of the cross," and said that he had never seen "so silly a production."

In 1834, the Assembly drew up a list of grievances and demands called the Ninety-Two Resolutions. Their basic demand called for control of the government by the Assembly. Papineau warned Britain that if the Ninety-Two Resolutions were not accepted, French Canadians would refuse to buy British-

■ Louis-Joseph Papineau led the rebellion in Lower Canada.

FURTHER UNDERSTANDING

Château Clique A clique is a group which is exclusive. Cliques do not readily welcome others to join them, particularly those who do not share their ways and views. This clique often visited the governor's home, called the Château St-Louis. As a result, they became known as the Château Clique. The most powerful group in Lower Canada, many of its members were appointed to the Executive and Legislative Councils. Members included British merchants and wealthy French merchants who supported the British. They were often granted special privileges by the government, such as land grants.

Doric Club The Doric Club was founded in 1836 in Montréal. The club consisted of young English-speaking **Tories**. This paramilitary political organization was opposed to the threat of French rule in Lower Canada.

Les Fils de la Liberté *Les Fils de la Liberté*, which means "sons of liberty" in the French language, was founded by about 700 Patriotes in 1837. The organization, which had political and military divisions, was inspired by the American Revolution and believed in the right of the people to choose their own government.

made goods and would remove their money from British banks. He even hinted at rebellion. Since Papineau's supporters won 87 percent of the seats in the Assembly that year, it was obvious that many people agreed with him.

The Assembly waited almost three years for its answer. In 1837, the British government issued the Ten Resolutions—its answer to the Assembly's demands. Britain refused each of the Assembly's requests and strengthened the governor's powers. Papineau responded with a call for a **boycott** of all tea, sugar, wine, linen, and leather goods imported from Britain. He encouraged Lower Canadians to smuggle goods from the United States.

The Rebellion Begins

Following the Ten Resolutions, French Canadians held protest meetings each week for three months. Young French Canadians formed a group called *Les Fils de la Liberté*

and began practising military drills without weapons. Early in November 1837, a street fight broke out in Montréal between members of the English-speaking group, the Doric Club, and *Les Fils de la Liberté*. An English-speaking mob surrounded Papineau's house in Montréal and began throwing stones. Papineau and his family were rescued by British troops. When Papineau learned that the governor was planning to arrest him and the other Patriote leaders, he quietly left town.

The first armed resistance took place at St-Jean. Several soldiers were returning to Montréal with two arrested Patriotes when the soldiers were ambushed and the Patriotes rescued. The rebellion had begun. As one Patriote told Papineau, "The ball is commenced. We must all take our place in the dance." Soon, the Patriotes began printing their own money. They also designed a flag and wrote a declaration of independence.

Les Fils de la Liberté clashed with the English-speaking Doric Club on the streets of Montréal in 1837.

A Quick DEFEAT

On November 23, 1837, Patriotes led by Dr. Wolfred Nelson defeated a British force at the village of St-Denis. This victory encouraged the French Canadians in the Richelieu Valley to volunteer for the Patriote cause. However, there were very few guns available. Two days later, British troops overwhelmed the Patriotes at St-Charles, killing thirty-five rebels.

By this time, Papineau and some rebel leaders had fled to the United States. The government offered $4,000 for Papineau's capture.

In December, 600 Patriotes fortified themselves in the village church of St-Eustache. Led by Sir John Colborne, a British army of 2,000 soldiers attacked, set fire to the church, and shot all those trying to escape. The village was burned. One newspaper wrote that "for a radius of 15 miles around St-Eustache not a building escaped being ravaged and pillaged by these new vandals." This battle marked the end of the rebellion in Lower Canada.

The government banned sixteen Patriote leaders—including Papineau— from Canada. Patriote supporters had their property looted and destroyed.

Suspected rebels were rounded up, tried, and sent to jail. Eight hundred Patriotes were jailed. Of the ninety-nine prisoners sentenced to death, twelve were hanged, fifty-eight were banished to prison colonies in Bermuda and Australia, and the rest were set free.

In February 1838, the British government suspended the province's constitution. The governor was ordered

■ After the battle at St-Charles, Patriote leaders retreated into the woods. While Louis-Joseph Papineau escaped, Dr. Wolfred Nelson was captured and jailed before he could leave Canada.

FURTHER UNDERSTANDING

Constitution A constitution is the organization and basic ideas upon which a government is based. By halting the constitution of Lower Canada, and restructuring their government to remove the power of the Patriote-composed Assembly, the British government hoped to regain order and control.

Dr. Wolfred Nelson Dr. Wolfred Nelson was a Patriote, whose mother was a Loyalist and whose father was born in England. As a young man, he detested Roman Catholics and French Canadians. After living among French Canadians he changed his views and supported the Patriotes in their fight against government abuses. The death of a close friend at the hands of British troops cemented his beliefs. In 1837, he led the rebels at the battle of St-Denis.

to rule Lower Canada with the help of the councils and without the Assembly.

A second rebellion broke out in November 1838. Within one week, the uprising was defeated by local volunteers. Shortly after, Papineau left Canada for exile in Paris, France. In the six battles of both uprisings, 325 men were killed. Of these, only 27 were soldiers, while the rest were rebels.

The rebellion in Lower Canada failed for several reasons. The poorly armed Patriotes were no match for the well-trained British troops. The Patriotes' strategy was poor and they lacked an overall plan. By the time they decided to use force, the government was well-prepared. There was also disagreement within the party, due to the fact that many of the moderate Patriotes did not want to use violence. To make matters worse, Papineau fled early in the fighting.

In addition, opposition from the Roman Catholic church limited the number of French Canadians who volunteered. The priests warned the French Canadians that those who took up arms would be **excommunicated** from the church. Finally, the Patriotes did not receive help from the United States because American President Van Buren did not wish to risk a war with Britain.

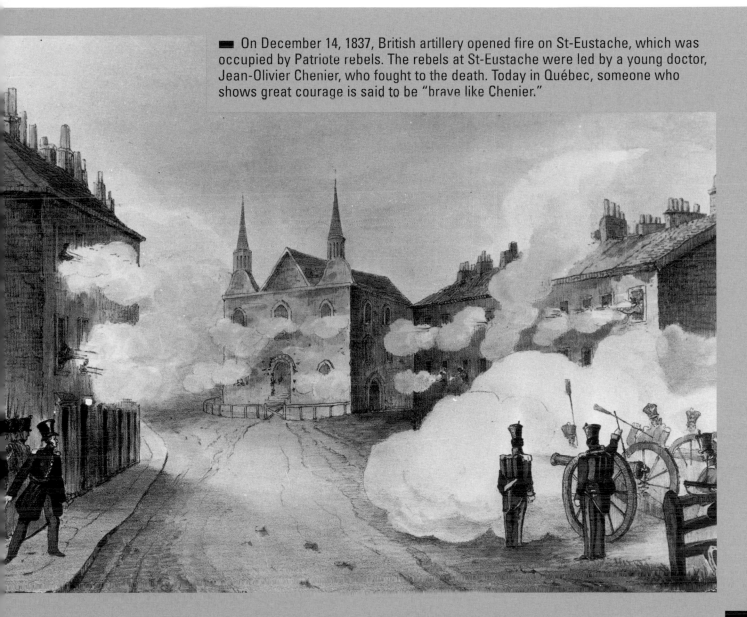

■ On December 14, 1837, British artillery opened fire on St-Eustache, which was occupied by Patriote rebels. The rebels at St-Eustache were led by a young doctor, Jean-Olivier Chenier, who fought to the death. Today in Québec, someone who shows great courage is said to be "brave like Chenier."

Upper Canada and the
FAMILY COMPACT

This group of Toronto families controlled the government and all the important jobs in the colony.

The beginning of the rebellion in Upper Canada followed a similar course to that of Lower Canada. At the time, a small group of people controlled the government of Upper Canada. They sat on both the Legislative and the Executive Councils. They were able to obtain good jobs for their friends and families through their influence over the lieutenant-governor. Since many of these individuals were related, they came to be known as the Family Compact.

The Family Compact consisted of about thirty people in present-day Toronto, then known as York. They all had served against the Americans during the War of 1812. Only a few members of the Family Compact were merchants, but they all promoted canals, trade, settlement, and banks. They were mostly civil servants, doctors, and lawyers. The members of the Family Compact believed in the superiority of the British Empire, British political institutions, and the Church of England. They shared a common dislike of democracy—especially American political ideas and institutions—and a distrust of common people. They also placed great importance on obedience of authority. As one member of the Family Compact said, the leaders of society and the government should be "gentlemen of high character, large property, superior information, intelligence, and loyalty."

This small group of Toronto families controlled the government and the important jobs in the colony. Outside of York, the Family Compact had many supporters. These supporters formed their own informal political party and were called "Tories." Between 1824 and 1836, the Tories won half of all elections.

FURTHER UNDERSTANDING

Elections Early elections provided great entertainment for pioneer settlements. An election continued for several days to allow enough time for everyone to vote. Wooden platforms were built in the largest villages and voters climbed onto the platform to shout out the name of the man they supported. Sometimes, party supporters fought to gain control of the platform to prevent the other side from voting. Many elections ended in wild brawls, precipitated by candidates who attempted to bribe voters with whisky. Heated discussions often ended in fights. One infamous election brawl took place near Belfast, Prince Edward Island, in 1847. Mobs of Irish and Scottish tenants attacked each other with clubs, fists, and boots. When election officials attempted to assist the victims, they were also beaten. At least three people were killed, while many others were wounded.

■ Colonel John By directed the construction of the Rideau Canal, which was completed in 1832. The canal joined Bytown, present-day Ottawa, with Kingston.

JOHN STRACHAN

The leader of the Family Compact was John Strachan. Strachan was born into a middle-class family in Scotland in 1778. At the age of 21, he crossed the Atlantic Ocean and settled in Cornwall, Upper Canada. There, he tutored the sons of some Loyalist families. Strachan was an outstanding teacher, and soon he was instructing the sons of the families that dominated government, business, and the professions. He taught his students to be loyal British subjects, good Christians, and patriotic to their own country.

When he first arrived in Upper Canada, Strachan was a **Presbyterian**. Since most of the leaders of the colony belonged to the Church of England, Strachan became an Anglican minister. Later in his career, he became the first Anglican bishop of Toronto.

The War of 1812 was the turning point in Strachan's career. He had just moved to York when the Americans captured the city. Strachan joined the party that rowed out to the American ships and arranged the terms of surrender. Strachan delayed the meeting long enough for the Canadians to hide their weapons and personal belongings before the Americans entered the city. Strachan then assumed leadership of the city. This experience convinced Strachan that it was his destiny to ensure Upper Canada remained British. After the war, he attempted to rid the colony of democratic and American influences.

John Strachan fought against the separation of church and state. He believed the Anglican church should play a major role in politics and education.

Strachan quickly moved up the social and political ladders. He helped to found the University of Toronto. During the cholera epidemics, Strachan showed no fear of death. He tended the sick, attended funerals, and raised people's spirits. The citizens of Toronto awarded him a silver vase in appreciation of his bravery.

In politics, Strachan became the unofficial leader of the government. The governor appointed him to the Executive Council in 1817, and to the Legislative Council in 1820. Many of his former pupils also sat on these councils and had senior posts in government.

William Lyon MACKENZIE

Although William Lyon Mackenzie was not the leader of the Reform Party, he became the most reknowned Reformer due to his role in the rebellion in Upper Canada in 1837. Mackenzie was born in Scotland in 1795. In 1820, he came to Upper Canada and started a newspaper—the *Colonial Advocate*.

Mackenzie was fiery in both looks and personality. He stood only 1.65 metres tall, and had bushy eyebrows and piercing blue eyes. Sometimes in a heated argument he would snatch the red wig from his head and hurl it at his opponent. His admirers called him "Little Mac." He was also called "The Firebrand."

Mackenzie did not like the way Upper Canada was being governed. In his first editorial, he wrote that the colony would never get ahead if it was run by an inactive governor who was surrounded by favourites, and who was represented by an easily corrupted Assembly. In one newspaper article he criticized the governor, the members of the two councils, and the Assembly.

Mackenzie was especially harsh on members of the Family Compact. In 1826, sons of several Family Compact members

FURTHER UNDERSTANDING

Francis Bond Head Sir Francis Bond Head was born in Britain in 1793. He became lieutenant-governor of Upper Canada in late 1835. While he was initially welcomed by the Reformers, his practices soon saw him fall out of favour. Hostilities escalated between the two camps. Bond earned votes by claiming that voting for Reformers would mean that Upper Canada would become part of the United States.

Reformers The main complaints of the Reformers in Upper Canada were that the Family Compact ignored public opinion, reserved the best jobs for its friends, controlled the economy for its own profit, and favoured the Anglican Church. Influenced by democratic movements in Britain, Europe, and the United States, the Reform Party sought to make government more democratic.

■ William Lyon Mackenzie was called a "muckraker" and "scandal-monger" by his enemies. There was even a failed assassination attempt on Mackenzie that was arranged by a prominent member of the Family Compact.

became so annoyed with Mackenzie's views that they broke into his office, smashed his press, and threw it into the harbour. The outcome of this event was opposite to what the vandals had anticipated. Mackenzie took them to court and won his case, making him even more popular. In 1828, Mackenzie was elected to the Assembly, where the Reformers now had a majority. Mackenzie was removed from the Assembly four times for slander, but each time the people re-elected him. In 1834, he was elected the first mayor of Toronto.

A Crisis in Upper Canada

In the Assembly, Mackenzie joined other Reform leaders, such as Dr. William Baldwin and his son, Robert. The Baldwins opposed violence and sought political change through peaceful means. They wanted responsible government, which meant that the Executive and Legislative Councils would be responsible to the elected Assembly.

The conflict between the Assembly and the councils developed into a crisis in 1836. When Lieutenant-Governor Francis Bond Head refused to consult the Reform Party—which dominated the Assembly—the entire Assembly resigned. During the election that followed, he accused the Reformers of being disloyal to Britain. He used bribery and violence to win votes. As a result, the Reformers were defeated, and many gave up politics altogether.

In 1837, the economy worsened. Poor crops and food shortages made many people more willing to listen to radical ideas. William Lyon Mackenzie took the lead. Rebellion loomed.

■ William Lyon Mackenzie used his printing press to make his 500-page *Report on Grievances* that demanded a number of changes, including responsible government and lower stamp prices. In 1826, the sons of several Family Compact members smashed his equipment and threw it into the harbour.

THE FIGHTING Begins

Mackenzie wore several overcoats, buttoned under the chin, thinking they would protect him from bullets.

The rebellion in Upper Canada was influenced by the uprising in Lower Canada. The lieutenant-governor sent regular troops stationed in Upper Canada to help fight the rebels in Lower Canada. William Lyon Mackenzie decided to strike while the troops were away. He planned to capture the city hall, take the arms stored there, and overthrow the government. The rebels set up their headquarters in Montgomery's Tavern, just north of Toronto.

On December 5, 1837, about 700 grim-faced men marched down Yonge Street toward Toronto. Only a few men carried muskets—most were armed with pitchforks and clubs. Mackenzie wore several overcoats, buttoned under the chin, thinking they would protect him from bullets. Church bells in Toronto sounded the alarm. For several days, rumours had circulated that the city was to be attacked by rebels. As they marched down the road, some of the rebels panicked when they saw what looked like a cannon being towed toward them. When the cannon turned out to be a wagon-load of sawn wood, the march continued.

Instead of marching directly into Toronto—which was unprotected—Mackenzie stopped to eat, and to negotiate with a truce party. When the lieutenant-governor learned how poorly armed and few in number the rebels were, he decided not to compromise, and raised a volunteer militia of about 250 men.

Confrontation at Montgomery's Tavern

In the growing darkness of late afternoon, the rebels met about twenty men led by Sheriff Jarvis. The sheriff's men fired one volley at the larger rebel force, then turned and ran. The rebels in the front rank fired their muskets, then dropped to the ground to reload and allow the men behind them

■ During the Battle of Montgomery's Tavern, William Lyon Mackenzie's battle cry was "Up then, brave Canadians! Get ready your rifles, and make short work of it!"

to fire over their shoulders. Thinking that the men in the front rank had been shot, the remaining rebels fled back to Montgomery's Tavern.

That night, the lieutenant-governor's reinforcements arrived. Two days later, the lieutenant-governor and 1,500 men confronted about 500 rebels at Montgomery's Tavern. The troops fired a cannon ball through the window of the tavern, causing panic among the rebels. The battle lasted only thirty minutes before the rebels—including Mackenzie—fled for their lives. They left behind Mackenzie's papers, which included a list of his supporters. The troops burned Montgomery's Tavern to the ground.

Although the governor offered a $4,000 reward for Mackenzie's capture, his supporters helped him escape across the border to the state of New York.

Mackenzie tried to keep the rebellion alive by establishing a government on Navy Island in the Niagara River. He offered free land to everyone who joined him. From here, the rebels launched several small raids into Upper Canada. In 1838, the rebels were defeated. The rebellion was officially over.

Following the Rebellion

The rebellion had failed. More than 880 people were jailed on suspicion of treason. Two of Mackenzie's supporters were hanged, ninety-two were deported, and twenty-six were banished from Canada. Hundreds of other Reformers fled the country to escape punishment.

The Tories were left in firm control of Upper Canada. The radical Reformers had lost the support of the people. Moderate Reformers, such as Robert Baldwin, became the new leaders of the Reform Party. Meanwhile, everyone waited to learn what actions Britain would take as a result of the rebellion.

RESULTS OF THE REBELLIONS

Some historians trace the origins of French-Canadian separatism to the Rebellion of 1837 in Lower Canada. French Canadians never forgot the Patriotes. One result of the rebellion was that the French-Canadian middle class lost prestige. Their promised victory had led to defeat, exile, and death. Moderate French Canadians took the lead in politics. These people were willing to work for economic progress. Many people turned to the church for support. As a result, the Roman Catholic church emerged as the unopposed leader of French-Canadian society.

A relatively small portion of the people of Upper and Lower Canada had actively supported the rebellions— perhaps as little as 1 percent of the population. In fact, most people supported the idea of reform within the context of the British structures of government. In Upper Canada, people were afraid that they might be accused of being a rebel if they challenged existing structures and ideas.

News of the fighting in the Canadas shocked the British government. Before the rebellions, few people in Britain took much interest in British North America, or knew that many people in the colonies were unhappy with their government. To investigate the problems, the British government sent Lord Durham to Canada to examine the situation and make suggestions on how to solve the problems.

THE REBELLIONS
in the Canadas

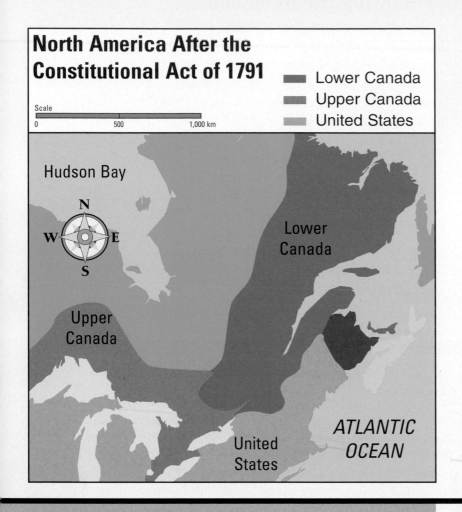

North America After the Constitutional Act of 1791

- Lower Canada
- Upper Canada
- United States

Scale
0   500   1,000 km

Hudson Bay

N
W   E
S

Lower Canada

Upper Canada

United States

ATLANTIC OCEAN

UPPER CANADA

Governments are formed by the Constitutional Act of 1791.

They are representative, but not responsible governments.

LOWER CANADA

TIME LINE

1834 The Parti Patriote draws up the Ninety-Two Resolutions asking for responsible government.

1837 Britain responds to the Ninety-Two Resolutions with the Ten Resolutions, which strengthen the councils.

1837 A series of crop failures and food shortages over the past few years make people willing to explore radical solutions.

November 1837 Rebellion in Lower Canada begins. The Patriotes declare independence and win an early victory at St-Denis.

November 1837 Troops are sent to fight rebels in Lower Canada. Mackenzie decides to rebel while the troops are away.

Government dominated by the Family Compact	**Reform Party led by William Lyon Mackenzie and the less radical Baldwins**
By the 1830s, many people were discontented with the government and the elites that controlled them.	Political parties demanded reform. When nothing was done to appease them, the radical elements of the parties became more influential.
Government dominated by the Château Clique, a group of mainly British merchants	**Parti Patriote led by Louis Joseph Papineau**

December 1837 Rebels in Upper Canada march down Yonge Street to take over the city hall. The rebels are defeated two days later at Montgomery's Tavern.

December 1837 The Patriotes are defeated at St-Eustache. Rebellion in Lower Canada ends.

February 1838 Britain suspends the constitution in Lower Canada and orders the governor to rule without elected representatives.

■ Execution of Patriote Rebels

Lord Durham ARRIVES

Reform newspapers were closed, and the threat of arrest hung over the heads of many Reformers.

When Lord Durham arrived in Lower Canada in May 1838, he found the colony in turmoil. Its jails were filled with captured Patriotes. A fair trial seemed impossible, since a British jury would find all the prisoners guilty and a French jury would set them all free. French–British hatred ran so high that violence could erupt again at any moment.

Conditions in Upper Canada were not much better. The rebels were defeated, and many of their leaders had left the country. The remaining rebels were either jailed or being closely watched. Reform newspapers were closed, and the threat of arrest hung over the heads of many Reformers. The economies of both colonies were suffering.

Immediate remedies were needed. First Durham cleared the jails. Rebels who had fled to the United States, notably Mackenzie and Papineau, were forbidden to return to Canada on threat of death. Durham exiled eight Patriote leaders to Bermuda and pardoned the remainder.

FURTHER UNDERSTANDING

Lord Durham John George Lambton, also known as Lord Durham, belonged to one of the richest families in Britain. Since he supported the idea of giving more people the vote, Durham was nicknamed "Radical Jack." Durham was an intelligent and talented person. He was also ambitious, independent, hot-tempered, and humourless. He did not work well with other people.

Durham had been the ambassador to Russia for two years. In 1837, he was on his way home when the British prime minister began to fear that Durham's presence in Britain might defeat his government. The rebellions in the Canadas provided the British prime minister a good excuse to send Durham to the colonies. Radical Jack became the governor general of British North America. He was instructed to discover the causes of the two rebellions and suggest solutions.

■ Lord Durham promised to heal the wounds caused by the rebellions.

Durham's Observations

Durham spent five months in British North America. Most of that time was spent in Lower Canada. He decided that the rebellion of Lower Canada had been more than a simple protest against an unfair system of government. Durham felt the cause of unrest originated in the power struggle between the French and British peoples. He said, "I expected to find a contest between a government and a people; I found two nations warring in the bosom of a single state."

Lord Durham did not understand how deeply French Canadians in Lower Canada treasured their language and traditions. He found the people cheerful, polite, and honest, but felt that they were too uneducated to govern themselves. He also thought the French Canadians could easily be misled by troublemakers such as Papineau.

Durham believed that British ways were superior to French ways. As a result, he concluded that the Assembly was to blame for the political problems in Lower Canada. Durham believed the British members of the two councils only wanted economic progress.

In Upper Canada, Durham blamed the Family Compact for the rebellion. He agreed with the complaints of the Reformers that the Anglican Church had too much power. He also agreed that the citizens should have more say in their own government.

Durham returned to Britain and completed his report about the Canadas for the British government in 1839. He died in July of the next year, without seeing the results of his well-known report.

■ Lord Durham freed many of the jailed rebels who had been charged with treason.

Durham's REPORT

Durham thought the most important problem to solve was the friction between British and French Canadians.

Durham's solution became the basis for the present system of government in Canada. His three primary recommendations, as contained in his *Report on the Affairs of British North America*, were:

- unite Upper and Lower Canada into one province,
- separate British affairs from local Canadian affairs, and,
- grant responsible government.

Durham believed the most important problem to solve was the friction between British and French Canadians. Since he believed that British ways were superior to French ways, Durham recommended that the French Canadians be assimilated. He thought that the union of the two colonies would solve the French–British conflict in Lower Canada. In a united province, the English-speaking Canadians would be a majority. French Canadians would not have the political power to oppose business

development along the St. Lawrence River. Durham hoped that by living side-by-side with the British, the French would learn the English language and British lifestyle. They would lose their sense of identity as a separate people. With an English-speaking population in control, it would be safe to grant self-government to the province.

Durham recommended that each colony be allowed to make laws that concerned its own local affairs. Britain should only control larger issues such as the colony's constitution and its relations with other countries.

Durham recommended that members of the Executive Council be chosen from the party with the majority of seats in the Assembly. If these individuals lost the support of the Assembly, they would be replaced by members who had its support. Regarding all local matters, the governor should abide by the wishes of the Executive Council. In this way, the people making the laws would be responsible to the Assembly, which in turn was responsible to the voters.

FURTHER UNDERSTANDING

Report on the Affairs of British North America In his report, Durham expressed support for responsible government. He felt that the Executive Council must have the confidence, or the support, of the majority of the Assembly. In addition, he suggested that the United Province of Canada should become more independent of the British government:

If [the British government] *has to carry on the Government in unison with a representative body, it must consent to carry it on by means of those in whom that representative body has confidence … I admit that the system which I propose would, in fact, place the internal government of the Colony in the hands of the colonists themselves; and that we should thus leave to them the execution of the laws.*

■ Queen Victoria ascended to the British throne at the age of 18 years. Her first official ceremonial act as monarch was to grant Durham his knighthood.

Act of UNION

The British government only accepted part of the Durham Report. While Britain decided to unite Upper and Lower Canada, it did not grant responsible government. In the Act of Union of 1840, Upper and Lower Canada became the United Province of Canada. Unofficially, Upper Canada was called Canada West, and Lower Canada became Canada East.

The government of the new United Province of Canada consisted of a governor general, an appointed Executive Council, an appointed Legislative Council, and an Assembly of elected representatives. At first, Parliament was located in Kingston, then it was moved to Montréal. Finally, it alternated between Kingston and Québec City.

Although the population of Canada East was 670,000, compared to 480,000 in Canada West, both regions received forty-two representatives in the Assembly. The British government planned to assimilate the French Canadians, so did not want them to control the government. In addition, the Act of Union banned the French language from official government usage and restricted French-Canadian educational institutions and civil law.

Britain decided to unite Upper and Lower Canada.

■ The first united Parliament sat in Kingston in July 1840.

FURTHER UNDERSTANDING

Kingston Kingston was once an important French fort and trading post called Fort Frontenac. In 1783, following the American Revolution, Kingston was settled by Loyalists and renamed King's Town, in honour of King George III. Soon, Kingston developed into the largest settlement in Upper Canada. Kingston's location at the intersection of Lake Ontario and the St. Lawrence River played an important role in its early development. However, with the arrival of the railway and larger shipping vessels, Kingston's importance diminished.

REFORMERS in the New Union

Reformers in both parts of the new colony pressed for responsible government.

Britain may have decided against responsible government for the United Province of Canada, but the matter was far from resolved. The next eight years saw reformers in both parts of the new colony pressing for responsible government. Their primary opposition came from the governors sent from Britain, the Family Compact in Canada West, and the Château Clique in Canada East.

In Canada West, Reform leader Robert Baldwin realized he needed the support of French-Canadian members in Canada East. Without their support, he would never be able to force the government to accept political change. Baldwin made friends with Louis-Hippolyte LaFontaine, the leader of the French-Canadian Reformers. When LaFontaine was defeated in the 1841 election, Baldwin arranged for him to be elected in Canada West. When the first governor general, Lord Sydenham, refused to appoint LaFontaine, along with other French Canadians, to the Executive Council, Robert Baldwin resigned from the council.

Sydenham died in 1841 from lockjaw after falling from his horse. Knowing that he required French-Canadian support to continue in government, the new governor general, Sir Charles Bagot, appointed LaFontaine to the Executive Council. LaFontaine accepted the position with the condition that Baldwin and other Reformers also be appointed. Bagot agreed.

Bagot died in 1843. The new governor general, Sir Charles Metcalfe, would not listen to Reformer demands. He refused to seek the approval of the Executive Council before making appointments. As a result, all but one council member resigned. For the next four years, the Reformers and the Tories fought for control of the Assembly, and the governor refused to consider responsible government.

■ The united Parliament was moved to Montréal in 1844. The capital would eventually move to Toronto, Québec City, and finally Ottawa in 1857.

FURTHER UNDERSTANDING

Alliance Individuals or groups who agree to join together are forming an alliance. They agree to co-operate in order to achieve a common purpose. Sometimes political parties join in a coalition. This is a form of alliance in which the parties formally agree to work together in order to achieve a common goal. Two parties might agree to work together temporarily in order to gain power and to control government.

TWO REFORMERS MAKE AN ALLIANCE

Louis-Hippolyte LaFontaine

Louis-Hippolyte LaFontaine was born in Lower Canada in 1807. He was educated in Montréal. He began a career as a lawyer in 1828 and was first elected to the Assembly in 1830. LaFontaine was a follower of Papineau until 1837, when they disagreed about the use of violence. LaFontaine travelled to London to plead for reform. Back in Canada, he was arrested in 1838, but was released without a trial. At this time, he became the leader of the moderate forces for reform in Lower Canada.

LaFontaine knew that the Act of Union was designed to assimilate the French Canadians. By co-operating with Canada West Reformers like Baldwin to achieve responsible government, LaFontaine and other French-Canadian moderates could use their share of political power to protect their culture.

LaFontaine insisted on speaking French in the Assembly, even after Britain outlawed it in 1839. Eventually his persistence led Britain to remove the restriction. LaFontaine's administration reformed many government institutions. He left politics in 1851 and became the chief justice in 1853. He was made a baronet by Queen Victoria and a papal knight by the Pope in 1854.

Louis-Hippolyte LaFontaine

Robert Baldwin

Robert Baldwin was born in Toronto in 1804. His father, William, was a wealthy landowner, lawyer, and Reform politician in the Assembly. The Baldwins were Anglicans, and Robert received his early schooling from John Strachan. Robert entered politics in 1829, more out of a sense of public duty than personal interest. While he was not a natural leader, his fellow Reformers and Tories respected the way he kept strictly to his principles. He resigned several times from his elected office to avoid supporting a decision he did not believe was right.

Baldwin believed in responsible government. When William Lyon Mackenzie turned to violence in 1837, the governor selected Robert Baldwin to meet with the rebels and offer a truce. Later, Baldwin defended several Reformers in court. When Durham visited Upper Canada, the two Baldwins met with him. They had earlier written Durham about the advantages of responsible government and may have influenced his recommendation in the report.

Robert Baldwin

Responsible Government AT LAST

In 1846, Britain adopted free trade. It was no longer important for Britain to maintain economic control over the Canadian economy. Consequently, there was no reason not to grant the colonies more control over their own affairs. Lord Grey, who was placed in charge of all the British colonies, appointed Durham's son-in-law, James Bruce, the Earl of Elgin, the governor general of the United Province of Canada.

Lord Elgin arrived in Canada in 1847. He was eager to put responsible government into practice. His chance came after the 1848 election, when the Reform party won the majority of the seats in both sections of the colony. Elgin asked Reform leaders Robert Baldwin and Louis LaFontaine to appoint the Executive Council. They suggested members of their own party. Lord Elgin agreed. Responsible government had arrived. The first real test of responsible government came in 1849.

Rebellion Losses Bill

In 1849, LaFontaine presented a bill to the Assembly called the Rebellion Losses Bill. It was designed to pay Lower Canadians for losses suffered during the rebellion of 1837. Upper Canadians had already been awarded damages. The bill angered many British merchants in Canada East. They called it a payment for rebellion. In fact, one Patriote claimed $50,000 for damages the British troops had done to his property.

The issue raised passions on both sides. During debate in Parliament one day, the guards had to clear the galleries when a brawl broke out among the spectators. Another time, the Assembly sat continuously for twenty-four hours trying to outlast the shouts and whistles from the galleries. In Toronto, a likeness of Robert Baldwin, who supported the bill, was burned in the streets. One English-language newspaper declared that

FURTHER UNDERSTANDING

Free trade A sytem of free trade involves the exchange of goods between countries. Trade is permitted without taxes, duties, or restrictions imposed by the government.

Prior to British adoption of free trade, Canadian wheat, flour, and timber had a guaranteed market in Britain. Wheat, flour, and timber exported from every country, except Canada, were taxed when they entered Britain. In the mid-1840s, Britain removed the taxes. Canada's products now had to compete on an equal basis with goods from around the world.

■ To mark the 100th anniversary of responsible government in Canada, a commemorative stamp was issued on October 1, 1948.

"as long as there is one axe and rifle on the frontier and British hands to wield it, these claims will not be passed."

Since the Reform party controlled the Assembly, the bill was passed. It was sent to Lord Elgin to be signed. The Tories, the Family Compact, and the Château Clique put pressure on Lord Elgin not to sign the bill. Personally, Lord Elgin did not approve of the bill, but his advisers in the Executive Council favoured it.

While Elgin believed in the principles of responsible government, the thought of possible violence was disturbing. Elgin's wife, Mary, was expecting a baby. Her doctors had ordered complete rest and quiet. Suppose a mob attacked the governor's mansion? On the other hand, Mary was Durham's daughter, and she strongly believed in her father's political ideas. She urged her husband to sign the bill.

LORD ELGIN'S DILEMMA

If Lord Elgin signed the bill, it would please its supporters, anger its opponents, and support responsible government. However, if he chose not to sign the bill, it would anger its supporters, please its opponents, and fail to support responsible government.

There were several different reactions to the bill. The French-Canadian moderates would have said: "If funds are given to pay for losses during the rebellion, it would prove that the French community is considered an equal partner in the United Province of Canada."

The Reformers in Canada West would have said: "A similar bill was passed in Upper Canada. This is a test of responsible government. If it is the will of the people, the bill should be signed."

The British merchants in Canada East would have said: "We are angry. Paying people for their losses is rewarding them for rebelling against Britain."

The Family Compact would have said: "Elgin should not sign the bill. We risk losing our influence in the Assembly to the French Canadians."

■ On March 10, 1848, Lord Elgin called upon the members of the majority to form the government. It is a date often referred to as "the birth of democracy in Canada."

RIOTS in Montréal

Parliament was still in session when the mob burst into the building.

Lord Elgin signed the Rebellion Losses Bill in 1849. As he left Parliament House in Montréal, an angry crowd pelted him with dead rats, stones, and rotten eggs. Infuriated by the signing of the bill, a mob of British Canadians marched toward the government buildings. Parliament was still in session when the mob burst into the building. The mob smashed the lights, ripped down wall hangings, and destroyed furniture. When a fire broke out in the west wing, Assembly members quickly voted to adjourn. They quietly walked out as the Parliament buildings burned to the ground.

The mob controlled the streets for several days. It sacked LaFontaine's property, cut down his fruit trees, burned his stable, and destroyed his furniture. Soldiers arrived before the mob could burn down his new house.

Rioting continued in Montréal for four months. Violent protests erupted in Toronto and other cities in Canada. Likenesses of Elgin and LaFontaine were burned in the streets. Angry crowds threw vegetables, dead rats, and garbage at members of the Assembly.

FURTHER UNDERSTANDING

Annexation Manifesto

Annexation occurs when a smaller country is joined with a larger country—sometimes without permission. The Annexation Manifesto explained the viewpoints of the Montréal merchants:

Of all the remedies that have been suggested for the acknowledged and insufferable ills with which our country is afflicted, there remains but one to be considered ... This remedy consists in a friendly and peaceful separation from the British connection and a union upon equitable terms with the [United States].

Within the Annexation Manifesto, they also outlined what they believed would be the benefits of such a union. They believed that land values would go up in Canada, that economic interaction with Britain would not likely be damaged, and that economic interaction would increase with other countries. They also predicted the growth of railroad systems. Overall, they felt that both the United States and Canada would benefit.

Bytown

Philemon Wright came from Massachusetts, in 1800, to settle near the Ottawa River. He constructed a sawmill and started a lumber business in what is now Hull, Québec. Following the War of 1812, Colonel John By was sent to organize the building of the Rideau Canal. This would provide a travel route that avoided American territory. The community across the river from Wrightstown (Hull) grew as canal workers moved to the area. Bytown, name after Colonel By, became the centre of the lumber industry. When it became a city in 1855, its name was changed to Ottawa.

■ Although Lord Elgin refused to call in the military to quell the Montréal riots, he did not hesitate to refer to the city as being "rotten to the core."

The riots came to an end, but many people were still unhappy. Some British Canadians believed that the government was controlled by French Canadians. Free trade with Britain had ruined many Canadian merchants, and the resulting economic depression made them even more angry with the British government.

Late in 1849, more than 300 well-known Montréal businessmen proposed that Canada join the United States. The proposal was outlined in a written document, called the Annexation Manifesto. The following year, another annexation group formed in Toronto. This movement never received much support, and when the economy improved a year later, the annexation movement died.

A NEW CAPITAL

One of the most debated issues in the United Province of Canada was which city should be the capital. Between 1841 and 1849, the Assembly voted 218 times on this issue. Britain selected Kingston as the colony's first capital. Although Kingston's population was only 8,000, the British government believed that Toronto and Montréal would be difficult to defend against an attack from the United States, and Québec City was surrounded by French Canadians who were unhappy with the union.

In 1844, the Reform-dominated Assembly felt that Kingston was too conservative. It chose Montréal as the site for the capital. When the Parliament buildings burned down in 1849, the capital moved to Toronto.

Afterward, the capital alternated every two years between Toronto and Québec City. In 1857, Queen Victoria, advised by the Canadian government, chose Bytown—now called Ottawa—as the permanent capital. It was midway between Canada East and Canada West. It was safe from attack and was populated by French and British inhabitants.

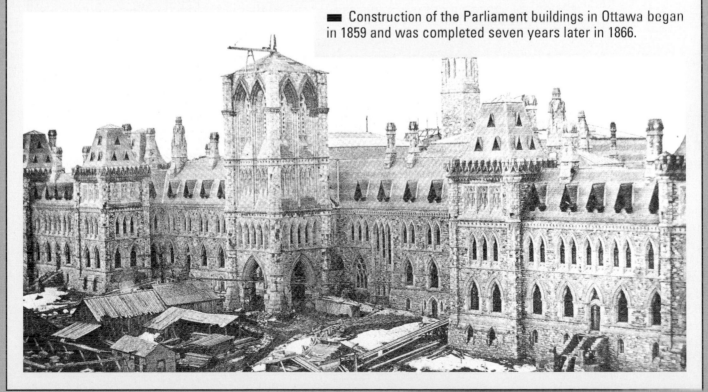

■ Construction of the Parliament buildings in Ottawa began in 1859 and was completed seven years later in 1866.

A Peaceful Solution in the
MARITIMES

There were no rebellions in the Maritimes as there were in Upper and Lower Canada. The governments of the Maritime colonies were dominated by wealthy merchants and landowners who ruled more for their own benefit than did the Family Compact in Upper Canada. Most Maritimers were farmers, fishers, tradespeople, or lumberjacks. The Maritimes did not have to deal with the French–British conflict that divided the people of Lower Canada, and there was little of the anti-American feeling that troubled Upper Canada. As a result, reformers had less trouble getting the government to listen to their complaints. They achieved responsible government with little or no violence.

Nova Scotia

In Nova Scotia, Joseph Howe boasted that responsible government was achieved "without a blow struck or a pane of glass broken." Britain granted Nova Scotia responsible government in 1848.

New Brunswick

Under Reform leaders Charles Fisher and Lemeul A. Wilmot, New Brunswick also received responsible government in 1848. New Brunswick's population was relatively uniform. The majority of the people were Loyalists and Anglicans. None of the violence that had erupted in the Canadas was to be felt here.

Prince Edward Island

Prince Edward Island's Family Compact owned or controlled most of the land in the colony. These landlords prevented their tenants from owning their own land. The Assembly sought responsible government so that it could force the landlords to sell

■ By 1827, the population of Newfoundland was more than 60,000.

their land to the tenants. Under George Coles and Edward Whelan, Prince Edward Island received responsible government in 1851.

Newfoundland

Newfoundland received its first council in 1824. The members of the council were important merchants from St. John's. They were mostly British Protestants. In 1832, Britain allowed the island to vote for the Assembly. The Assembly represented the majority of the population, who were poor Irish Roman Catholic fishers. As a result of the conflict between Catholic and Protestants, Irish and British, and rich and poor, the elections were often violent. To end the violence, Britain suspended the Assembly from 1840 until 1847. It was not until 1855 that Newfoundland obtained responsible government, under Reform leaders Philip Little and John Kent.

JOSEPH HOWE

In 1835, Joseph Howe, the editor of the *Novascotian* newspaper, published a letter in his newspaper exposing the dishonesty of several Halifax judges. He was charged with libel and was swiftly brought to trial. Howe skillfully conducted his own defence. Speaking to a packed courtroom, he exposed the unfair methods that taxes were passed, and spoke out against judges who foreclosed on the poor. He described the injustices of the governmental system. Howe held the courtroom spellbound for more than six hours. At times, the audience roared with laughter, and the judge was forced to call for order. At other times, people were reduced to tears. The jury declared Howe not guilty. After the verdict, the excited crowd hoisted him to their shoulders and carried him home. Howe's popularity as a champion of the poor helped him become elected to the Assembly in 1836.

Like the Reformers in Upper and Lower Canada, Howe pushed for responsible government. He once declared:

"In England, the people can breathe the breath of life into their government whenever they please. In this country, the government is like an ancient Egyptian mummy, wrapped up in narrow and antique prejudices, dead and inanimate, but yet likely to last forever."

Howe saw responsible government established in Nova Scotia in 1848.

Joseph Howe was the leader of the Nova Scotian Reformers.

Economic CHANGES

The railways ushered in a new age of heavy industry and urban growth.

The 1840s and 1850s witnessed many important economic changes. The loss of protected markets in Britain, as a result of their adoption of free trade, and a worldwide economic depression in 1847, slowed trade.

By 1850, trade improved—especially in grain and timber. During the 1830s, the governments of the Canadas improved roads and built a series of canals that linked the Great Lakes with Montréal. In the 1850s, there was a boom in railway construction. Soon, tracks linked the larger cities in the United Province of Canada with cities in the United States. The railways ushered in a new age of heavy industry and urban growth.

In 1854, the United States signed the Reciprocity Treaty with the British North American colonies. As a result, exports to the United States of timber, grain, coal, fish, and livestock increased. Trade in grain, flour, and timber jumped from $8 million in 1854 to $16 million the next year.

In 1857, the Canadas adopted the American system of decimal currency. The modern post office system also began during these years. The Canadas, Nova Scotia, and New Brunswick printed their first stamps in 1851. By 1861, each colony had its own stamps.

In the Atlantic Colonies

From the late 1700s to the mid-1800s, the Atlantic colonies attracted English, Irish, and Scottish immigrants—those looking to escape uncertain economic circumstances, those with ties to the fishing or timber industries, and those seeking land or a new beginning. They participated in the labour force of the region's developing industries. In the 1800s, the timber industry and, in turn, the shipbuilding industry grew and prospered—particularly in Nova Scotia and New Brunswick. The Newfoundland fishing industry doubled between 1785 and 1815, with exports such as dried cod.

Britain kept watch on the colonies, closely regulating their trading activities. The colonies traded almost exclusively

■ Alexander Mackenzie was the first person to cross North America north of the Mexican border. He relied heavily on voyageurs and Aboriginal guides on his journey.

FURTHER UNDERSTANDING

Decimal currency In the 1850s, there was a debate in Canada over whether the colony should follow the British money system, which used pounds, shillings, and pence, or adopt the American system of dollars and cents. Since trade with the United Sates had increased greatly, it was decided to adopt the the American system, known as decimal currency, since it is based upon units of ten. In decimal currency 1 dollar equals 100 cents.

Reciprocity Treaty This agreement between Britain and the United States, in effect between 1855 and 1866, allowed for the free trade of natural resources and products between British North America colonies and the United States. For example, the colonies could trade wheat to Americans without having to pay **tariffs**.

with Britain. They exported timber and fish products in exchange for British goods, such as salt and tea. Merchants emerged in the colonies to assist the process. Eventually, trade spread to other areas in Britain's empire, such as the West Indies. Some minerals were also sold to British markets. Prince Edward Island and Nova Scotia, produced farm products, such as livestock and grain, for export and for local food markets. New Brunswick was strong in timber trade and shipbuilding. By the time Britain withdrew its trade protection in the 1840s, the economy of the Atlantic region was established to an extent that it was able to survive independently.

THE FUR TRADE IN THE 1800s

Fur traders in Montréal joined together in 1783 to form the North West Company. They built a trading centre on Lake Superior called Fort William to help supply their posts in the West. To compete, the Hudson's Bay Company also built inland trading posts. By 1795, however, the North West Company controlled more than two-thirds of the fur trade.

Explorers such as Alexander Mackenzie, Simon Fraser, and David Thompson pushed further west. More and more posts were built, and the rivalry between the North West Company and the Hudson's Bay Company intensified in the early 1800s. With trading posts spread out east to west, and north, the competition ended in 1821. The two companies joined under the name the Hudson's Bay Company. As other industries, such as timber, grew, the importance of the fur trade declined.

■ The fur trade played a crucial role in the exploration and development of early Canada.

■ Canada's first railway was the Champlain and St. Lawrence Railway, which ran through the lumbertown of Bytown. It officially opened in 1836.

The Road to RESPONSIBLE GOVERNMENT

1791 The Constitutional Act grants representative government with limited powers for elected representatives. The act divides Québec into Upper and Lower Canada.

1812 Americans invade Canada and are successfully repelled by an alliance of Aboriginal, British, and Canadian forces, led by Sir Isaac Brock.

1838 The British government suspends Lower Canada's constitution. The governor and councils are in charge, but there is no Assembly.

1839 Lord Durham completes his *Report on the Affairs of British North America*. He recommends uniting Upper and Lower Canada into one province, separating British from local affairs, and granting responsible government.

■ The Death of Sir Isaac Brock

1837–8 Rebellions erupt in Upper and Lower Canada as people become discontented with their lack of power in government.

1840 The Act of Union unites the provinces, but does not grant responsible government.

1840 Newfoundland's Assembly is suspended due to violence during elections.

1838–1846 Reformers in both parts of the United Province of Canada ask for

■ Battle at St-Charles

42

responsible government. Louis-Hippolyte LaFontaine and Robert Baldwin form an alliance to press for reform.

1846 Britain adopts free trade and no longer has reason to prevent Canada from governing its own affairs.

1847 Britain sends Lord Elgin, the son-in-law of Lord Durham, to Canada to act as governor general.

1847 Newfoundland is granted its Assembly again.

1848 Responsible government is granted in Nova Scotia and New Brunswick "without a blow struck or pane of glass broken."

1848 The Reform Party wins a majority in the election. Elgin asks Baldwin and LaFontaine to appoint the Executive Council. Responsible government is in place.

1849 LaFontaine presents the Rebellion Losses Bill to the Assembly. The Assembly passes the bill.

1849 Lord Elgin signs the bill even though he does not support it, thereby entrenching responsible government in Canada.

1851 Prince Edward Island achieves responsible government.

1855 Newfoundland is granted responsible government.

Joseph Howe's Court Victory

QUIZ

(answers on page 47)

Multiple Choice

Choose the best answer in the multiple choice questions that follow.

1 Which was not a reason for the rebellion in Upper Canada?

a) the Upper Canadian troops had been sent to Lower Canada to control its rebellion

b) Reformers felt that the Family Compact kept the best jobs for their friends

c) the Legislative Council often ignored the wishes of the democratically elected Assembly

d) the habitants were suffering from a series of crop failures that made it difficult for them to feed their families

2 Why were the British merchants discontented with life in Lower Canada before the rebellion?

a) they believed the habitants did not grow as much wheat as they should

b) the French Canadians dominated the Assembly

c) they wished to build canals and pay for them by taxing farmland

d) all of the above

3 Who was not an important player in the rebellions?

a) William Lyon Mackenzie King

b) Louis-Joseph Papineau

c) Dr. Wolfred Nelson

d) William Lyon Mackenzie

4 Which was not one of Lord Durham's recommendations?

a) unite Upper and Lower Canada into one province

b) strengthen the power of the Legislative Council

c) grant responsible government

d) separate British affairs from local Canadian affairs

5 What was the main reason that Britain finally granted responsible government to the United Province of Canada?

a) Louis-Hippolyte LaFontaine and Robert Baldwin convinced them with a report to the British government

b) Britain believed another rebellion might break out in the colony if they did not grant responsible government

c) Britain adopted free trade and no longer had a reason to control colony affairs

d) Lord Elgin convinced the British government to make the change shortly after his arrival in Canada

6 Which individual(s) used newspapers as an important means of spreading their ideas?

a) Louis-Joseph Papineau

b) Joseph Howe

c) William Lyon Mackenzie

d) b) and c)

Mix and Match

Match the description in column A with the correct terms in column B. There are more terms than descriptions.

A

1. The body of government in Upper and Lower Canada that was representative
2. The outspoken leader of the Reform Party in Upper Canada
3. The articulate leader of the Nova Scotian Reformers who pushed for responsible government
4. A proposed law designed to pay Lower Canadians for the losses they suffered during the 1837 rebellion
5. A group of new immigrants to Québec that inspired Britain to divide Québec into Upper Canada and Lower Canada
6. A group of merchants who ruled Lower Canada in their own interests

B

a) Loyalists
b) Assembly
c) Québec Act
d) Family Compact
e) William Lyon Mackenzie
f) Joseph Howe
g) Château Clique
h) Lord Elgin
i) Rebellion Losses Bill

Time Line

Find the appropriate spot on the time line for each event listed below.

A Rebellion strikes in Upper and Lower Canada.

B Nova Scotia and New Brunswick are granted responsible government.

C Upper and Lower Canada combine to form the United Province of Canada.

D Upper and Lower Canada are created by the Constitutional Act.

E Lord Durham completes his report on British North America.

F A cholera epidemic strikes Lower Canada.

1791 **1**	1820 William Lyon Mackenzie arrives in Canada and starts the *Colonial Advocate*	1837 **3**
1801 French Canadians dominate the Assembly in Lower Canada		1838 Rebellions end. Britain suspends constitution of Lower Canada
1812 The War of 1812 increases loyalty and pride of Canadian citizens	1831 Mackenzie is elected mayor of Toronto	1839 **4**
	1832 **2**	1840 **5**
1815 Louis-Joseph Papineau becomes leader of the Parti Patriote	1833 Major crop failure in Lower Canada	1848 **6**
	1836 More crop failure in Lower Canada	1851 Prince Edward Island is granted responsible government
1817 John Strachan appointed to the Executive Council in Upper Canada	1836 The Tories win the election	1855 Newfoundland is granted responsible government
	1837 Crop failures hit both Canadas	

Conclusion

The Constitutional Act of 1791 was Britain's attempt to help the French and British co-exist in British North America. When the United States attacked Upper Canada in the War of 1812, the British and French came together to fend off the Americans, but French–British conflicts continued.

Unrest in Upper and Lower Canada developed. The Parti Patriote in Lower Canada objected to the power of the Château Clique, whose members controlled the councils. Reformers in Upper Canada were fed up with the Family Compact. In 1837, rebellions occured in Upper and Lower Canada. The British defeated the rebels. However, the British government sent Lord Durham to investigate. His report recommended uniting the Canadas into one province, separating the British from local affairs, and granting responsible government. The Act of Union united the Canadas in 1840. Responsible government was not established until 1849, and was put to the test when Lord Elgin signed the Rebellion Losses Bill.

In 1855, British North America included five provinces: The United Province of Canada—composed of Canada East and Canada West—Prince Edward Island, Nova Scotia, New Brunswick, and Newfoundland. Each province had representative and responsible governments. They would face many decisions as they considered nationhood and looked toward the West.

Further Information

Suggested Reading

Berton, Pierre. *Flames Across the Border: 1813–1814.* Toronto: Doubleday Canada, 2001.

Craig, Gerald M. (Ed.) *Lord Durham's Report.* Montéal: McGill-Queen's University Press, 1963.

Francis, Douglas, Richard Jones, and Donald B. Smith. *Origins: Canadian History to Confederation.* Toronto: Harcourt Canada, 2000.

Sugden, John. *Tecumseh: A Life.* New York: Owl Books, 1999.

Suthren, Victor. *War of 1812.* Toronto: McClelland & Stewart, 2001.

Internet Resources

Canada: A People's History Online
history.cbc.ca
The online companion to CBC's award-winning television series on the history of Canada, as told through the eyes of its people. This multimedia Web site features behind-the-scenes information, games, puzzles, and discussion boards. The site is also available in French.

The Canadian Encyclopedia Online
www.thecanadianencyclopedia.com
A reference for all things Canadian. In-depth history articles are accompanied by photographs, paintings, and maps. All articles can be read in both French and English.

Glossary

aide-de-camp: a military officer who functions as an assistant to a higher-ranking officer

Anglican Church: the Church of England; includes those churches in other countries that follow the doctrines of the Church of England

boycott: refusal to have anything to do with someone or something

British North America: the name given to the remaining British colonies in North America, following the American Revolution

conservative: the political position that opposes change in favour of traditional views and values

direct democracy: form of democracy in which every individual participates in the assembly and may vote on each issue

excommunicated: having one's membership to a church or religious group cut off

franchise: a privilege or right granted by a government

Presbyterian: member of the Presbyterian Church, which is a Protestant branch of Christianity that follows the teachings of John Calvin

quarantine: enforced isolation to prevent the spread of infectious disease

seigneuries: the name given to sections of farmland in French Canada

suffrage: the right to vote

tariffs: a tax placed on imported or exported goods

Thirteen Colonies: the former British colonies in what is now the United States; includes Connecticut, Delaware, Georgia, Maryland, Massachusetts, New Hampshire, New Jersey, New York, North Carolina, Pennsylvania, Rhode Island, South Carolina, and Virginia

Tories: a British term for people who favour conservative political policies

wheat rust: a destructive disease that affects wheat; caused by a rust fungus

Answers

Multiple Choice	Mix and Match	Time Line
1. d)	1. b)	1. d)
2. d)	2. e)	2. f)
3. a)	3. f)	3. a)
4. b)	4. i)	4. e)
5. c)	5. a)	5. c)
6. d)	6. g)	6. b)

Index